I0448621

Congressional Research Service
Informing the legislative debate since 1914

Generalized System of Preferences: Background and Renewal Debate

Vivian C. Jones
Specialist in International Trade and Finance

May 19, 2014

Congressional Research Service

7-5700

www.crs.gov

RL33663

Summary

The U.S. Generalized System of Preferences (GSP) program provides non-reciprocal, duty-free tariff treatment to certain products imported from designated beneficiary developing countries (BDCs). The United States, the European Union, and other developed countries have implemented similar programs since the 1970s.The U.S. program was first authorized in Title V of the Trade Act of 1974, and is subject to periodic renewal by Congress. The GSP program was most recently extended until July 31, 2013, in Section 1 of P.L. 112-40, and has not yet been renewed. Imports under the GSP program in 2013 amounted to about $18.5 billion—about 7% of all imports from GSP countries, and about 1% of total U.S. imports.

The expiration of GSP means that renewal of the program may continue to be a legislative issue in the second session of the 113th Congress. In recent years, GSP renewal has been somewhat controversial. For example, in past years some Members reportedly asserted that more "advanced" developing countries, such as Brazil and India, should not receive benefits under U.S. preference programs, and proposed ending or limiting their benefits in favor of providing a greater share of benefits to eligible least-developed beneficiaries. Other Members have proposed expanding preferences to grant duty-free, quota-free access (DFQF) to all least-developed countries. Last year, in the first session of the 113th Congress, controversy arose over funding provisions in Senate bill S. 1331 seeking to renew GSP. Other GSP legislation in the 113th Congress includes H.R. 2709, H.R. 2139, and H.R. 1682.

The GSP program is one of several U.S. trade preferences through which the United States seeks to help developing countries expand their economies. Other U.S. trade preference programs are regionally focused, and include the African Growth and Opportunity Act (AGOA), the Andean Trade Preference Act (ATPA), and the Caribbean Basin Initiative (CBI). The GSP program provides duty-free entry for over 3,500 products (based on 8-digit U.S. Harmonized Tariff Schedule tariff lines) from 127 beneficiary developing countries (BDCs) and territories, and duty-free status to an additional 1,500 products from 44 GSP beneficiaries that are additionally designated as least-developed beneficiary developing countries (LDBDCs).

U.S. implementation of GSP requires, first, that eligible countries conform to certain criteria, including taking steps to maintain internationally-recognized worker rights; and reducing trade-distorting investment policies and practices, among other things. Second, in order to receive GSP benefits, at least 35% of the appraised value of the product must be the "growth, product, or manufacture" of the BDC. Third, the GSP program includes certain curbs on product eligibility intended to shield U.S. manufacturers and workers from potential adverse impact due to the duty-free treatment. These include specific exclusion of certain "import sensitive" products (e.g., textiles and apparel), and automatic limits on the quantity or value of any one product imported under the program (products from least-developed beneficiaries are not subject to this restriction). Fourth, GSP country and product eligibility are subject to annual review.

This report presents, first, recent developments and a brief history, economic rationale, and legal background leading to the establishment of the GSP. Second, the report presents a discussion of U.S. implementation of the GSP. Third, the report presents an analysis of the U.S. program's effectiveness and the positions of various stakeholders. Fourth, implications of the expiration of the U.S. program and possible options for Congress are discussed.

Contents

Figures

Tables

Appendixes

Contacts

Introduction

The Generalized System of Preferences (GSP) program gives unilateral, nonreciprocal preferential tariff treatment to certain products imported from designated beneficiary developing countries (BDCs). The United States, the European Union, and other developed countries have implemented such programs since the 1970s in order to promote economic growth in developing countries by stimulating their exports.

The U.S. program (as established by Title V of the Trade Act of 1974) is subject to periodic renewal by Congress, and was last extended through July 31, 2013, in P.L. 112-40. GSP expiration means that program renewal, and possible reform, may continue to be a legislative issue in the second session of the 113th Congress.

Renewal of the GSP program has been somewhat controversial in recent years, and there has been considerable discussion in Congress about GSP reform. For example, some in Congress have asserted that certain "more advanced" developing countries (such as Brazil and India) are receiving GSP benefits so that least-developed countries (LDCs) are not receiving the maximum benefits and support possible.

This report presents, first, a brief summary of GSP developments and legislation introduced in the 113th Congress. Second, it provides a brief history, economic rationale, legal background, and comparison of GSP programs worldwide. Third, the report describes in more detail the U.S. implementation of the GSP program. Fourth, the report analyzes the U.S. program's effectiveness and stakeholder positions. Fifth, possible options for Congress are discussed.

Recent Developments

On July 17, 2013, a GSP renewal bill was introduced in the House, H.R. 2709, seeking to extend the preference until September 30, 2015. A related bill, S. 1331, was introduced in the Senate on July 18. Controversy reportedly arose in the Senate over funding of the GSP program, which was not resolved prior to the July 31 expiration date.[1] Thus, the program expired and has not yet been renewed.

Russia's GSP Status

Reportedly, there is congressional interest in renewing GSP, but a recent concern has arisen over Russia's status as a GSP beneficiary following its invasion of Crimea.[2] On May 7, 2014, President Obama notified Congress that he intends to graduate Russia from the GSP program because he has determined that "it is appropriate to withdraw Russia's designation as a beneficiary developing country under the GSP program because Russia is sufficiently advanced in economic development and improved in trade competitiveness that continued preferential

---

[1] Len Bracken, "Expiration of GSP Costly for Importers, No Immediate Resolution," *Bloomberg BNA International Trade Daily*, January 15, 2014.

[2] "Levin Says Efforts on GSP Renewal Hampered by Questions over Russia," *Inside U.S. Trade*, April 10, 2014.

treatment under the GSP is not warranted."[3] The President's withdrawal of the preference was based on section 502(f)(2) of the Trade Act of 1974 (19 U.S.C. 2462(f)(2)), which states that one of the factors determining country eligibility is its level of economic development (see "Eligible Countries," below).

In 2013, Russia was the ninth-largest beneficiary of the GSP by value, with goods totaling about $466 million receiving duty-free treatment under the preference; or about 2% of total Russian exports to the United States. Major U.S. imports from Russia under GSP in 2012 included ferrosilicon; chromium and ferrocromium; radial tires; ceramics for laboratory use; and aluminum wire, alloy bars, and rods.

In addition, according to U.S. laws implementing GSP, if a beneficiary "has become a 'high income' country, as defined by the official statistics of the International Bank for Reconstruction and Development [i.e., World Bank], then the President shall terminate the country as a beneficiary developing country ... effective on January 1 of the second year following which the determination is made."[4] Currently, a "high income" country is one with a gross national income (GNI) per capita of $12,616 or more.[5] According to World Bank data (see **Table 1**, below), Russia reached this "high income" threshold in 2012.

Table 1. Russia: Gross Domestic Product and Gross National Income per capita

(current U.S. dollars)

	2004	2005	2006	2007	2008	2009	2010	2011	2012
GDP per capita	$4,109	$5,337	$6,947	$9,146	$11,700	$8,616	$10,710	$13,284	$14,037
GNI per capita, Atlas method	$3,410	$4,460	$5,820	$7,590	$9,710	$9,290	$10,000	$10,810	$12,700

Source: World Bank World Development Indicators.

Notes: GDP = Gross Domestic Product; GNI = Gross National Income.

Russia's GSP eligibility was also reviewed by the GSP Subcommittee of the Trade Policy Staff Committee (TPSC) in the context of its 2012 GSP annual review, based on two "country practices" petitions (see "Annual Reviews" below). One petition, filed in 2011, by U.S. investors in the Yukos Oil Company, alleged that Russia expropriated the company without any compensation to the U.S. investors.[6] The second petition, originally filed in 2008, alleged that Russia does not adequately protect intellectual property rights (IPR)—another criterion that could have made Russia ineligible to receive GSP benefits. In the 2012 review (the most recent conducted to date), the GSP Subcommittee decided to continue investigating the IPR petition, and to defer a decision on acceptance of the expropriation petition.[7]

---

[3] U.S. Congress, House Committee on Ways and Means, *Withdrawal of Russia as a Beneficiary Developing Country under the Generalized System of Preferences*, Executive Communication from Obama, Barack H., 113th Cong., 2nd sess., May 7, 2014, H.Doc.113-107.

[4] 19 U.S.C. §2462(e).

[5] World Bank home page, "How We Classify Countries," http://data.worldbank.org/about/country-classifications.The World Bank's principal criterion for classifying economies is gross national income (GNI) per capita using an Atlas conversion factor.

[6] USTR, *Public Hearing for U.S. Generalized System of Preferences (GSP) Review of Country Practices*, March 28, 2013.

[7] USTR, "Results of the 2012 GSP Annual Review," see "Active and Pending GSP Country Practice Reviews," June (continued...)

Other Countries Recently Suspended from or Included in GSP

On June 27, 2013, the President announced the suspension of GSP benefits for **Bangladesh** on the grounds that "it has not taken or is not taking steps to afford internationally recognized worker rights to workers in the country."[8] The suspension became effective 60 days after the publication of the proclamation in the *Federal Register*, or Friday, August 30, 2013. According to administration trade officials who reviewed Bangladesh's progress, the country has made advances in some areas such as hiring more building inspectors and increasing union registrations; however, the country still comes short on labor law reforms related to freedom of association and collective bargaining.[9]

On March 26, 2012, President Obama suspended GSP benefits for Argentina because "it has not acted in good faith in enforcing arbitral awards in favor of United States citizens or a corporation, partnership, or association that is 50% or more beneficially owned by United States."[10] A list of GSP-eligible countries appears in **Appendix C**.

On March 26, 2012, the President designated the **Republic of South Sudan** as a least-developed beneficiary developing country under the GSP.[11] On June 29, 2012, the President designated Senegal as a least-developed beneficiary developing country, effective 60 days after the date of the proclamation (or September 27, 2012).[12]

113th Congress Legislation

Proposed legislation in the113th Congress includes

- H.R. 1682 (April 23, 2013, Lofgren) proposes to add Vietnam to the list of countries ineligible for GSP, unless the President certifies that Vietnam (1) is not on the special watch list of countries not in compliance with minimum standards for the elimination of human trafficking; (2) does not engage in pervasive violations of internationally-recognized human rights, including freedom of speech and freedom of religion; and (3) otherwise meets the GSP eligibility requirements.

- H.R. 2139 (May 28, 2013, Crenshaw) and related Senate bill S. 1839 (December 17, 2013, Begich) seeks to make certain luggage and travel articles in Harmonized Tariff Schedule (HTS) subheading 4202 eligible for GSP status.

- H.R. 2709 (July 17, 2013, Camp/Levin) seeks to extend GSP until September 30, 2015.

(...continued)

2013, http://www.ustr.gov/sites/default/files/2012%20AR%20Results%20List_0.pdf.

[8] Presidential Proclamation 8997 of June 27, 2013, 78 *Federal Register* 39949, July 2, 2013.

[9] Inside U.S. Trade, "U.S. to Make Initial Determination on Bangladesh GSP Status in June," April 24, 2014.

[10] Proclamation 8788 of March 26, 2012, 77 *Federal Register* 18899, March 29, 2012.

[11] Ibid.

[12] Ibid.

- S. 1331 (July 18, 2013, Baucus/Hatch) seeks to extend GSP until September 30, 2015. This bill would provide funding offsets by extending the merchandise processing fee until January 22, 2022, and the Consolidated Omnibus Budget Reconciliation Act (COBRA) fee until January 29, 2022. It also proposes to increase the amount of the required installment of estimated tax due in 2019 for certain corporations while reducing the amount due in following periods by the corresponding amount.⌐

- H.R. 3167 (September 20, 2013, Terry) seeks to prohibit GSP eligibility for countries that (1) failed to provide adequate protection for intellectual property rights (IPR); or (2) maintained local content requirements.

History, Rationale, and Comparison of GSP Programs

The basic principle behind each GSP program worldwide is to provide developing countries with unilateral preferential market access to developed-country markets in order to spur economic growth in poorer countries. The preferential access is in the form of lower tariff rates (or as in the U.S. case, duty-free) for certain products that are determined not to be "import sensitive" in the receiving country market. The program was first adopted internationally in 1968 by the United Nations Conference on Trade and Development (UNCTAD) at the UNCTAD II Conference.[13]

Economic and Political Basis

The GSP concept and programs were established based on an economic theory that preferential tariff rates in developed country markets could promote export-driven industry growth in lesser developing countries. It was believed that this, in turn, would help to free beneficiaries from heavy dependence on trade in primary products (e.g., raw materials), and help diversify their economies to promote stable growth.[14]

Some economists claim that GSP was established, in part, as a means of reconciling two widely divergent economic perspectives of trade equity that arose during early negotiations on the General Agreement on Tariffs and Trade (GATT).[15] Industrialized, developed nations argued that the most-favored-nation principle[16] (MFN) should be the fundamental and universal principle

---

[13] U.N. Conference on Trade and Development, "About GSP," at http://www.unctad.org. In addition to the United States and the European Union, eight other developed countries—Australia, Bulgaria, Canada, Japan, New Zealand, Norway, the Russian Federation, and Switzerland—currently have GSP programs.

[14] OECD Secretary-General. *The Generalized System of Preferences: Review of the First Decade*. Organization of Economic Cooperation and Development, 1983, p. 9 (hereinafter OECD GSP Review).

[15] Sapir, A. and L. Lundberg, "The U.S. Generalized System of Preferences and its Impacts," in R. Baldwin and A. Krueger (eds.) *The Structure and Evolution of Recent U.S. Trade Policy*, Chicago: The University of Chicago Press, 1984.

[16] The most-favored-nation principle means that countries must treat imports from other trading partners on the same basis as that given to the most favored other nation. Therefore, with certain exceptions (including GSP, regional trading arrangements, and free trade agreements), every country gets the lowest tariff that any country gets, and reductions in tariffs to one country are provided also to others. The term "most-favored-nation" has been changed in U.S. law to "normal trade relations."

governing multilateral trade, while less-developed countries believed that equal treatment of economically unequal trading partners did not constitute equity in trade benefits, and called for "special and differential treatment" for developing countries. These economists assert that GSP schemes thus became one of the means of offering a form of special treatment that developing nations sought, while allaying the fears of developed countries that tariff "disarmament" might create serious disruptions among import-sensitive industries in their domestic markets.[17]

Due to differences in developed countries' economic structures and tariff programs—as well as different domestic industries and products each wanted to shield from foreign competition—it proved difficult to create one unified system of tariff concessions on additional products. Therefore, the GSP became a system of individual national schemes based on common goals and principles—each with a view toward providing developing countries with generally equivalent opportunities for export growth.[18] As a result, the preference-granting countries implemented various individual schemes of *temporary, generalized, non-reciprocal, non-discriminatory* preferences under which tariffs were lowered or eliminated on some imports from certain developing countries.

As a condition for providing such tariff preferences, GSP preference-granting countries reserved the right to (1) exclude certain countries; (2) determine product coverage; (3) determine rules of origin governing the preference; (4) determine the duration of the scheme; (5) reduce any preferential margins accruing to developing countries by continuing to lower or remove tariffs as a result of multilateral negotiations; (6) prevent the concentration of benefits among a few countries; (7) include safeguard mechanisms or "escape" clauses to protect import-sensitive industries; and (8) place caps on the volume of duty-free trade entering under their programs.[19]

GATT/WTO Framework

Although GSP programs were intended to be temporary, an international framework under the GATT was developed to allow the programs to continue. By its very nature as a trade preference, the GSP program posed a problem under the GATT because the granting of preferences would be inconsistent with the fundamental obligation placed on GATT Parties (GATT Article I:1) to grant MFN tariff treatment to the products of all other GATT Parties. However, since preference programs were viewed as vehicles of future trade liberalization and economic development for developing countries, GATT Parties accommodated them in a series of joint actions.

First, in 1965, the GATT Parties added Part IV to the General Agreement, an amendment that recognizes the special economic needs of developing countries and asserts the principle of non-reciprocity. Under this principle, developed countries may forego the receipt of reciprocal benefits for their negotiated commitments to reduce or eliminate tariffs and restrictions on the trade of less developed contracting parties.[20] Second, because of the underlying MFN issue, GATT Parties in 1971 adopted a waiver of Article I for GSP programs, which allowed developed contracting parties to accord more favorable tariff treatment to the products of developing

---

[17] OECD GSP Review, p. 11.

[18] Ibid., p. 10.

[19] Wall, David. "Problems with Preferences," *International Affairs*, vol. 47, October 1971, p. 95.

[20] Edmond McGovern, International Trade Regulation ¶ 9.212 (updated 1999). Part IV is generally viewed as nonbinding, though some have argued otherwise with regard to certain of its provisions. *Id.*; John H. Jackson, William J. Davey & Alan O. Sykes, Jr., Legal Problems of International Economic Relations 1171 (4th ed. 2002).

countries for 10 years.[21] The GSP was described in the decision as a "system of generalized, non-reciprocal and non-discriminatory preferences beneficial to the developing countries."

Enabling Clause

At the end of the Tokyo Round of Multilateral Trade Negotiations in 1979, developing countries secured adoption of the so-called Enabling Clause, a permanent deviation from MFN by joint decision of the GATT Contracting Parties.[22] The clause states that notwithstanding GATT Article I, "contracting parties may accord differential and more favorable treatment to developing countries, without according such treatment to other contracting parties," and applies this exception to:

> (a) Preferential tariff treatment accorded by developed contracting parties to products originating in developing countries in accordance with the Generalized System of Preferences;

> (b) Differential and more favorable treatment with respect to the provisions of the General Agreement concerning non-tariff measures governed by the provisions of instruments multilaterally negotiated under the auspices of the GATT;

> (c) Regional or global arrangements entered into amongst less-developed contracting parties for the mutual reductions or elimination of tariffs and, in accordance with criteria or conditions which may be prescribed by the CONTRACTING PARTIES for the mutual reduction or elimination of non-tariff measures, on products imported from one another;

> (d) Special treatment on the least developed among the developing countries in the context of any general or specific measures in favour of developing countries.[23]

Additional Commitment to LDCs

When launching the Doha Development Agenda (DDA) negotiations in November 2001, World Trade Organization (WTO, established in 1995) members committed themselves to provide "duty free/quota free" (DFQF) access to the products of least-developed countries in keeping with the shared objective of the international community as expressed in the Millennium Development Goals.[24] During DDA negotiations at the sixth WTO Ministerial Conference in Hong Kong in December 2005, developed country WTO members and "developing country members declaring themselves in a position to do so" agreed to deepen this commitment by providing DFQF access to at least 97% of products originating from LDCs by 2008, or no later than the start of the implementation period (i.e., of any multilateral WTO agreement that might be reached), "in a

---

[21] GATT, Generalized System of Preferences; Decision of 25 June 1971, L/3545 (June 28, 1971), available at http://www.wto.org/gatt_docs/English/SULPDF/90840258.pdf.

[22] GATT, Differential and More Favourable Treatment, Reciprocity and Fuller Participation of Developing Countries; Decision of 28 November 1979, L/4903 (December 3, 1979)(footnotes omitted), available at http://www.wto.org/gatt_docs/English/SULPDF/90970166.pdf.

[23] For more information on the treatment of GSP and other preference programs in the WTO, see CRS Report RS22183, *Trade Preferences for Developing Countries and the World Trade Organization (WTO)*, by Daniel T. Shedd, Jane M. Smith, and Brandon J. Murrill.

[24] World Trade Organization, "The WTO and the Millennium Development Goals," http://www.wto.org/english/thewto_e/coher_e/mdg_e/mdg_e.htm.

manner that ensures stability, security and predictability."[25] As of 2011, 83.4% of all exports (excluding oil and arms) from LDCs entered into developed countries duty-free.[26] If the DDA were concluded, all developed country WTO members could be required to take on the DFQF commitment.

Comparison of International GSP Programs

Other developed countries besides the United States that have GSP programs are Australia, Bulgaria, Canada, the European Union (EU), Japan, New Zealand, Norway, the Russian Federation, and Switzerland.[27] One economist has referred to these programs as a non-homogeneous set of national schemes sharing certain common characteristics.[28] Generally, each preference-granting country extends to qualifying developing countries (as determined by each benefactor) an exemption from duties (reduced tariffs or duty-free access) on most manufactured products and certain "non-sensitive" agricultural products. Product coverage and the type of preferential treatment offered vary widely.[29]

Although most GSP schemes (including the U.S. program) admit all eligible products duty-free, some countries provide tariff reductions, rather than complete exemption from duties.[30] The Australian System of Tariff Preferences (ASTP), for example, is based on a five percentage point margin of preference. When the Australian General Tariff (GT) is higher than 5%, the ASTP tariff rate is reduced by 5% (for example, if the GT rate is 20%, the ASTP rate is 15%). When the GT rate is 5% or less, the ASTP rate is zero.[31]

In the WTO, the developing country status of members is generally based on self-determination. However, with regard to GSP, each preference-granting country establishes particular criteria and conditions for defining and identifying developing country beneficiaries. Consequently, the list of beneficiaries and exceptions may vary greatly between countries. If political or economic changes have taken place in a beneficiary country, it might be excluded from GSP programs in some countries but not in others. Most countries, including the United States, also exclude countries if they have entered into another kind of commercial arrangement (e.g., a free trade agreement) with any other GSP-granting developed country.

In terms of additional GSP product coverage for LDCs, the EU's program, which offers duty-free access for "everything but arms,"[32] is currently perhaps the most inclusive in terms of GSP-

---

[25] World Trade Organization, Ministerial Declaration, Annex F. December 18, 2005, WT/MIN(05)/DEC.

[26] United Nations Integrated Implementation Framework, *WTO Hong Kong DFQF Target*, http://iif.un.org/content/wto-hong-kong-dfqf-target.

[27] U.N. Conference on Trade and Development, "About GSP," at http://www.unctad.org.

[28] Sanchez Arnau, Juan C. *The Generalized System of Preferences and the World Trade Organization*. London: Cameron May, Ltd., 2002, p. 187.

[29] Ibid.

[30] World Trade Organization, Committee on Trade and Development. The Generalized System of Preferences: A Preliminary Analysis of the GSP Schemes in the Quad. WTO Document WT/COMTD/W/93, October 5, 2001.

[31] United Nations Conference on Trade and Development, Generalized System of Preferences on the Scheme of Australia. UNCTAD Technical Cooperation Project on Market Access, Trade Laws and Preferences, June 2000 (INT/97/A06), p. 5. http://www.unctad.org/en/docs/itcdtsbmisc56_en.pdf.

[32] European Communities, GSP Council Regulation (EC) No. 2501/2001. See also Council Regulation (EC) No 732/2008 of 22 July 2008 applying a scheme of generalised tariff preferences for the period from 1 January 2009 to 31 (continued...)

eligible products. GSP-granting countries may also have incentive-based programs that provide enhanced benefits for beneficiary countries that meet certain additional criteria. For example, in 2007, the European Community implemented a regulation that grants additional GSP benefits to those countries that have demonstrated their commitment to sustainable development and internationally- recognized worker rights.[33]

Each preference-granting nation also has safeguards in place to ensure that any significant increases in imports of a certain product do not adversely affect the receiving country's domestic market. Generally, these restrictions take the form of quantitative limits on goods entering under GSP. Under Japan's system, for example, imports of certain products under the preference are limited by quantity or value (whichever is applicable) on a first-come, first-served basis as administered on a monthly (or daily, as indicated) basis. For other products, import ceilings and maximum country amounts are set by prior allotment.[34] The United States quantitatively limits imports under the GSP program by placing "competitive need limit" (CNL) thresholds on the quantity or value of commodities entering duty-free, as discussed in more detail below.

Each GSP benefactor also has criteria for graduation—the point at which beneficiaries no longer qualify for benefits because they have reached a certain level of development. Most preference-granting countries require mandatory graduation based on a certain level of income per capita based on World Bank calculations. Some programs, such as the EU's, also specifically provide for graduation of certain GSP recipients with respect to individual sectors of the economy.

EU GSP Changes

On January 1, 2014, the EU implemented substantial changes to its GSP program that are intended to: (1) better focus on countries in need; (2) further promote core principles of sustainable development and good governance; and (3) enhance stability and predictability.[35]

The EU's revisions reduced GSP-eligible countries to 90, down from 176. The other 86 countries previously eligible were excluded because they: (1) had alternative trade arrangements for accessing the EU market; (2) had become high or upper-middle income countries; or (3) had other preferential arrangements with the EU.[36]

The EU also added additional tariff lines (mostly chemicals, fertilizers, and base metals) to the list of duty-free products eligible for GSP, narrowed certain countries' benefits to fewer products

---

(...continued)

December 2011 and amending Regulations (EC) No 552/97, (EC) No 1933/2006 and Commission Regulations (EC) No 1100/2006 and (EC) No 964/2007. Published in Official Journal of the European Communities, (OJ) OJ L 211 of 6 August 2008. The "Everything but Arms" provision applies to all goods except arms and munitions and white sugar (from October 1, 2009 to September 2012, sugar importers "shall undertake to purchase such products at a minimum price not lower than 90% of the reference price."). See Council Regulation (EC) No 2501/2001.

[33] Ibid.

[34] World Trade Organization, Committee on Trade and Development. *Notification by Japan,* June 21, 2000, WT/COMTD/N/2/Add.9.

[35] Regulation (EU) No. 978/2012 of the European Parliament and of the Council of 25 October 2012 Applying a Scheme of Generalized Tariff Preferences and repealing Council Regulation (EC) No. 732/2008, OJ L 303/1, October 31, 2012. See also European Commission, "Revised EU Trade Scheme to Help Developing Countries Applies on 1 January 2014," Memo, December 19, 2013, http://trade.ec.europa.eu/doclib/docs/2013/december/tradoc_152015.pdf.

[36] Ibid.

(e.g., China may only receive benefits for vegetable products; animal and vegetable fats and waxes; meat products; tobacco, and mineral products), and graduated certain competitive sectors in some GSP-eligible countries (e.g., Ukraine will not receive GSP benefits for railway and tramway vehicles and products).[37]

In order to add a measure of stability to the program, the EU extended GSP benefits for 10 years, and provided transition periods of at least one year for those countries that will lose GSP eligibility.

Future Canada Changes

Canada announced recently that, effective January 1, 2015, Canada's General Preferential Tariff (GPT) will be withdrawn from 72 countries.[38] GPT will continue to be available to 103 beneficiaries. Canada will continue to review the list of beneficiary countries biannually, and will automatically graduate countries that are either classified for two consecutive years as high income countries; or have a 1% or greater share of world exports for two consecutive years.[39]

United States GSP Implementation

Congress first authorized the U.S. Generalized System of Preferences scheme in Title V of the Trade Act of 1974 (P.L. 93-618), as amended.[40] P.L. 93-618 authorizes the President to grant duty-free treatment under the GSP for any eligible product from any beneficiary developing country (BDC) or least-developed beneficiary developing country (LDBDC), provides the President with economic criteria in deciding whether to take any such action, and also specifies certain other criteria for designating eligible countries and products.[41]

Based on the statutory requirements countries must meet while participating in the program, the U.S. GSP program might be characterized as both a foreign policy tool and an international trade program. Although GSP benefits are non-reciprocal, certain criteria speak to important U.S. commercial interests, such as ensuring "equitable and reasonable" access in the beneficiaries' market to U.S. products, protecting IPR, and preventing the seizure of property belonging to U.S. citizens or businesses. In addition, since certain import sensitive products are excluded from eligibility and quantitative/value limitations apply to eligible imports, the economic costs to competing U.S. industries of the preference are quite small.

---

[37] Ibid.

[38] Canada Gazette, "General Preferential Tariff Withdrawal Order (2013 GPT Review), Volume 147, No. 21, October 9, 2013.

[39] Ibid.

[40] Trade Act of 1974, P.L. 93-618, Title V, as amended, 19 U.S.C. §2461-2467. The GSP Program was reauthorized and amended by the Trade and Tariff Act of 1984 (P.L. 98-573), and again by Subtitle J (the GSP Renewal Act of 1996) of P.L. 104-188. Twelve laws have authorized GSP with relatively minor modifications, most recently through July 31, 2013 (P.L. 112-40). See **Table B-1**.

[41] 19 U.S.C. §2461.

Eligible Countries

When designating BDCs and LDBDCs, the President is directed to take into account certain mandatory and discretionary criteria. The law prohibits (with certain exceptions) the President from extending GSP treatment to certain countries, as follows:[42]

- other industrial countries (Australia, Canada, EU member states, Iceland, Japan, Monaco, New Zealand, Norway, and Switzerland are specifically excluded);

- communist countries, unless they are a WTO member, a member of the International Monetary Fund, and receive Normal Trade Relations (NTR) treatment from the United States; must also not be "dominated or controlled by international communism;"

- countries that collude with other countries to withhold supplies or resources from international trade or raise the price of goods in a way that could cause serious disruption to the world economy;

- countries that provide preferential treatment to the products of another developed country in a manner likely to have an significant adverse impact on U.S. commerce;

- countries that have nationalized or expropriated the property of U.S. citizens, or otherwise infringe on U.S. citizens' property rights, including patents, trademarks, or copyrights; countries that have taken steps to repudiate or nullify existing contracts or agreements of U.S. citizens (or corporations, partnerships, or associations that are 50% or more owned by U.S. citizens) in a way that would nationalize or seize ownership or control of the property; or countries that have imposed or enforced taxes or other restrictive conditions on measures on the property of U.S. citizens; *unless* the President determines that compensation is being made, good faith negotiations are in progress, or a dispute has been handed over to arbitration in the Convention for the Settlement of Investment Disputes or another forum;

- countries that have failed to act in good faith in recognizing as binding or in enforcing arbitral awards in favor of U.S. citizens (or corporations, partnerships, or associations that are 50% or more owned by U.S. citizens); and

- countries that grant sanctuary from prosecution to any individual or group that has committed an act of international terrorism, or has not taken steps to support U.S. efforts against terrorism.

Mandatory criteria also require that beneficiary countries:

- have taken or are taking steps to grant internationally recognized worker rights (including collective bargaining, freedom from compulsory labor, minimum age for employment of children, and acceptable working conditions with respect to minimum wages, hours of work, occupational safety and health); and

- implement their commitments to eliminate the worst forms of child labor.[43]

---

[42] 19 U.S.C. §2462.

[43] 19 U.S.C. §2462(b). The most recent amendments required the support of U.S. efforts against terrorism and (continued...)

The President has the authority to waive certain mandatory criteria if he determines that GSP designation of any country is in the national economic interest of the United States and reports this determination to Congress.[44]

The President is also directed to consider certain criteria as "factors affecting country designation":

- the country's expressed desire to be designated a beneficiary developing country for purposes of the U.S. program;

- the level of economic development of the country;

- whether or not other developed countries are extending similar preferential tariff treatment to the country;

- its commitment to a liberal trade policy;

- the extent to which it provides adequate protection of IPR;

- the extent to which it has taken action to reduce trade-distorting investment policies and practices, and to reduce or eliminate barriers to trade in services; and

- whether or not it has taken steps to grant internationally recognized worker rights.[45]

The law further authorizes the President, based on the required and discretionary factors mentioned above, to withdraw, suspend, or limit GSP treatment for any beneficiary developing country at any time.[46]

Reporting Requirements

The President must advise Congress of any changes in beneficiary developing country status, as necessary.[47] The President must also submit an annual report to Congress on the status of internationally recognized worker rights within each BDC, including findings of the Secretary of Labor with respect to the beneficiary country's implementation of its international commitments to eliminate the worst forms of child labor.[48]

Least-Developed Beneficiaries

The President is also authorized by statute to designate any BDC as a LDBDC, based on an assessment of the conditions and factors previously mentioned.[49] Although factors such as per

---

(...continued)

expanded the definition of internationally recognized worker rights (Section 4102 of P.L. 107-210). See also United States Trade Representative. *U.S. Generalized System of Preferences Guidebook*, December 2011, p. 19 (hereinafter USTR Guidebook).

[44] 19 U.S.C. §2462(b)(2).

[45] 19 U.S.C. §2462(c). op cit., p. 20.

[46] 19 U.S.C. §2462(d).

[47] 19 U.S.C. §2462(d)(3).

[48] 19 U.S.C. §2464.

[49] 19 U.S.C. §2462(a)(2).

capita income level, economic stability, and quality of life indicators (on which the United Nations-designated list of LDCs is based) are taken into account,[50] the U.S. Administration also assesses the level of compliance with other GSP statutory requirements and comments from the public (as requested in the *Federal Register*) before identifying a country as "least-developed" for purposes of the GSP.[51]

Country Graduation from GSP

The President may also withdraw, suspend, or limit the GSP status of a BDC if he determines that the country is determined to be sufficiently competitive or developed, as President Obama removed Russia's GSP eligibility.[52] *Mandatory* country graduation occurs when the BDC is determined to be a "high income country" as defined by official World Bank statistics, or as a result of a review of the BDC's advances in economic development and trade competitiveness.[53] On December 20, 2012, the President determined that St. Kitts and Nevis had become a "high income country" and terminated its GSP beneficiary status as of January 1, 2014.[54] The President made the same determination on June 29, 2012, with respect to Gibraltar and the Turks and Caicos (also effective January 1, 2014).[55]

Countries are also ineligible for GSP benefits if they formally enter into a bilateral trading relationship (such as a free trade agreement) with another developed country. Bulgaria and Romania were the last countries to become ineligible for this reason, effective for each of the countries when it became an EU Member State, or as of January 1, 2007 (Presidential Proclamation 8098, December 29, 2007).[56] Although not specifically required by the GSP statute, developing countries that enter into a free trade agreement (FTA) with the United States also lose GSP eligibility in favor of the reciprocal concessions granted by the FTA.[57]

Countries Potentially Eligible for GSP

On April 16, 2013, the United States Trade Representative (USTR) requested public comments and announced a public hearing on whether to add **Burma (Myanmar)** and **Laos** to the list of beneficiary countries under the GSP program.[58] Burma's GSP eligibility has been suspended since July 1989, but Laos has never been considered for GSP eligibility. A hearing was held on June 4,

---

[50] 19 U.S.C. §2462(c)(2).

[51] See 71 F.R. 43543.

[52] In this case, the discretionary eligibility criteria under 19 U.S.C. §2462(c)(2) applies.

[53] 19 U.S.C. §2462(e).

[54] Proclamation 8921 of December 20, 2012, 77 *Federal Register* 76799, December 28, 2012.

[55] Proclamation 8840 of June 29, 2012, 77 *Federal Register* 39885, July 5, 2012.

[56] 72 F.R. 459. USTR officially announced the graduation of Bulgaria and Romania on January 22, 2007 (72 *Federal Register* 2717). Croatia joined the EU on July 1, 2013, but its GSP graduation has not yet been formally announced by the President, possibly due to GSP expiration.

[57] The language removing GSP benefits appears in the legislation implementing the FTA. Colombia and Panama were the latest countries to lose GSP status for this reason. See Section 201(a)(2) of the United States-Colombia Trade Promotion Agreement (P.L. 112-42) and Section 201(a)(2) of the United States-Panama Trade Promotion Implementation Act (P.L. 112-43).

[58] 78 *Federal Register* 22593.

2013. Shortly thereafter, the GSP program expired, and thus no action by the TPSC or President Obama regarding their eligibility has been taken to date.

According to pre-hearing comments, some U.S. nongovernmental organizations (NGOs), including the U.S. Campaign for Burma, EarthRights International, and the AFL-CIO, asserted that Burma, although it has recently instituted new labor laws, has not sufficiently demonstrated its willingness to address forced labor and worst forms of child labor issues, or to grant freedom of assembly or collective bargaining. The lack of adequate workplace protections was also mentioned.[59] Organizations and individuals representing the retail industry were strongly in favor of Burma and Laos being granted GSP eligibility, saying that it would "help Myanmar and Laos to reach their full economic potentials by diversifying their markets and becoming more globally integrated."[60] The International Intellectual Property Alliance (IIPA), a private sector coalition of trade associations representing copyright-based industries, did not oppose the granting of GSP benefits for either Burma or Laos, but pointed out several areas where these countries may not fully qualify for GSP eligibility based on IPR protection criteria. The IIPA requested a review of Burma and Laos's progress in meeting these criteria one year after the President designates them as GSP beneficiaries.[61]

Eligible Products

The Trade Act of 1974 authorizes the President to designate certain imports as eligible for duty-free treatment under the GSP after receiving advice from the United States International Trade Commission (USITC).[62] "Import sensitive" products specifically excluded from preferential treatment include most textiles and apparel goods; watches; footwear and other accessories; most electronics, steel, and glass products; and certain agricultural products that are subject to tariff-rate quotas.[63] The lists of eligible products and the list of beneficiary developing countries are reviewed and revised annually by the GSP Subcommittee.[64] Any modifications to these lists usually take effect on July 1 of the following calendar year.[65]

In terms of product coverage, more than 3,500 products are currently eligible for duty-free treatment, and about 1,500 additional articles originating in LDBDCs may receive similar treatment. Leading GSP imports in 2013 included petroleum products, especially crude oil; car and truck tires; ferrosilicon; aluminum alloy plates, sheet, and strip; and car and truck tires.[66] See **Table A-1** for a list of leading GSP imports.

---

[59] GSP Country Eligibility Review – Burma, Docket ID: USTR-2013-0020. http://www.regulations.gov.

[60] Ibid. Statement of the Retail Industry Leaders Association (RILA).

[61] Ibid. Statement of the International Intellectual Property Alliance (IIPA).

[62] 19 U.S.C. §2463(a)(1).

[63] 19 U.S.C. §2463(b).

[64] The GSP Subcommittee is a sub-group of the Trade Policy Staff Committee, given jurisdiction over designating beneficiary countries and covered products in the GSP program in Executive Order 11846, 40 F.R. 14291, as amended.

[65] USTR Guidebook, p. 8.

[66] USTR Guidebook and, Appendix A.

Rules of Origin

Eligible goods under the U.S. GSP program must meet certain rules of origin (ROO) requirements in order to qualify for duty-free treatment. First, duty-free entry is only allowed if the article is imported directly from the beneficiary country into the United States. Second, at least 35% of the appraised value of the product must be the "growth, product or manufacture" of a beneficiary developing country, as defined by the sum of (1) the cost or value of materials produced in the BDC (or any two or more BDCs that are members of the same association or countries and are treated as one country for purposes of the U.S. law, see **Table C-1**), plus (2) the direct costs of processing in the country.[67]

Competitive Need Limits and Waivers

The law also establishes "competitive need limits" (CNLs) that require the President to automatically suspend GSP treatment for BDCs (LDBDCs and sub-Saharan beneficiaries are exempt) if imports of a product from a single country reach a specified threshold value ($160 million in 2013 and $165 million in 2014), or if 50% or more of total U.S. imports of a product entering under GSP come from a single country.[68]

CNL waivers may be granted on a case-by-case basis to be determined by certain criteria. In deciding whether to grant a waiver, the President must (1) receive advice from the USITC as to whether a U.S. domestic industry could be adversely affected by the waiver; (2) determine that the waiver is in the U.S. economic interest; and (3) publish the determination in the *Federal Register*.[69] The President is also required to give "great weight" to the extent to which the BDC opens its markets to the United States, provides internationally recognized worker rights, and protects IPR.[70]

In 2006, Congress amended the GSP law to limit Presidential CNL waiver authority for products from certain countries if the imported value of the a product from that country exceeded 15% of the value of all U.S. GSP imports of the product; the country had a per capita GDP of $5,000 or more as determined by World Bank statistics; or had exported a total value of a number of products under GSP that was more than 10% of the value of all GSP product imports.[71]

The amendment also urged the President's to revoke any CNL waiver in effect for five years or more if the exports of the product were in excess of 1.5 times of the specified dollar amount reflected in the CNL provision, or if the product exports exceeded 75% of the appraised value of total imports of the product into the United States in a given year.[72] Thus, CNL waivers have been generally limited in recent years.

---

[67] 19 U.S.C. §2463(a).

[68] 19 U.S.C. §2463(c)(2)(A). See also USTR Guidebook, p. 11.

[69] 19 U.S.C. §2463(d).

[70] 19 U.S.C. §2463(d)(2).

[71] 19 U.S.C. §2463(d)(4)(b).

[72] Ibid.

De Minimis CNL Waivers

De minimis CNL waivers may also be provided if the total imported into the United States of a particular product from *all countries* is small. The *de minimis* level is adjusted each year, in increments of $500,000; for example, in 2013, the *de minimis* amount was $21.5 million, and is $22 million in 2014.[73]

CNL Waivers for Articles not Produced in the United States on January 1, 1995

Specific products that the President determined were not produced in the United States on January 1, 1995 are also exempt from CNLs. This type of waiver is also known as a "504(d)" waiver, and imports of these products may enter the U.S. duty-free from BDCs, unless imports of one of these products from the beneficiary country exceed 50 % of all U.S. imports of the product; or unless imports of the product exceed a specific dollar value set by the law ($160 million in 2013, increasing by $5 million each year). If either threshold is reached, duty-free access for that product is terminated on July 1st of the next calendar year.[74]

Annual Reviews

Although all GSP actions are made at the discretion of the President, the GSP program is administered by the GSP Subcommittee of the Trade Policy Staff Committee (TPSC), an executive branch interagency body chaired by the USTR that includes representatives from the Departments of Agriculture, Commerce, the Interior, Labor, State, and the Treasury.[75] The GSP Subcommittee makes annual recommendations to the President concerning continued country and product eligibility.

The GSP Subcommittee also resolves questions regarding BDCs' and LDBDCs' observance of country practices (such as worker rights or IPR protection); investigates petitions to add or remove items from the list of eligible products; and considers which products should be removed on the basis that they are "sufficiently competitive" or "import sensitive" relative to U.S. domestic firms. In preparation for the annual review, the USTR may also seek an investigation by the USITC for the purpose of providing advice concerning any possible modifications to the GSP.[76]

2012 Annual Review Results[77]

The annual review of the GSP program for 2012 was completed in June 2013, and the President implemented his decisions on GSP country and product eligibility in Presidential Proclamation

---

[73] 19 U.S.C. §2463(c)(2)(F). These waivers are automatically reviewed by the GSP Subcommittee (see below), but are granted at the discretion of the President.

[74] 19 U.S.C. §2463(c)(2)(E). The TPSC GSP Subcommittee automatically considers *de minimis* waivers each year. Granting waivers is a discretionary decision of the President. See USTR Guidebook, p. 12.

[75] Regulations for implementation of the GSP program were issued by the Office of the United States Trade Representatives at 15 C.F.R. §2007. Provisions for the GSP Annual Review are set out at 15 C.F.R. §2007.2(c)-(h).

[76] 19 U.S.C. §1332(g), 19 U.S.C. §2463.

[77] 78 *Federal Register* 40822.

8897 of June 27, 2013.[78] Results of the annual review included the suspension of Bangladesh from GSP due to a long-standing worker rights investigation, and the postponement of a decision on a request from Ecuador that sought to add certain cut flowers and vegetables to the list of products eligible for GSP status.[79]

Pending 2013 Review

Since GSP expired on July 31, 2013, all activities of the GSP Subcommittee are on hold. However, on July 29, 2013, the USTR announced deadlines for any submissions for the 2013 GSP review. On November 22, 2013, the USTR extended the deadline for CNL waiver petitions in context of the 2013 review. In each case, the USTR reported that no action would be taken on the petitions if the program remained without authorization, but requested the petitions "so that the President can be in a position to take action if Congress acts to reauthorize the GSP program."[80]

Effectiveness of GSP

The statutory goals of the GSP are to (1) promote the development of developing countries; (2) promote trade, rather than aid, as a more efficient way of promoting economic development; (3) stimulate U.S. exports in developing country markets; and (4) promote trade liberalization in developing countries.[81] It is difficult to assess whether or not the program alone has achieved these goals, however, because the GSP is only one of many such foreign aid initiatives used by the United States to assist poorer countries. Economic success within countries is also related to internal factors, such as governance, stability, wise policy decisions, availability of infrastructure to foster industry, and legal/financial frameworks that encourage foreign investment.

What follows, therefore, are general comments, rather than hard data, about the impact of GSP on developing countries, and possible economic effects on the U.S. market. The positions of various stakeholders regarding the value of the program are also discussed.

Effects on Developing Countries

In the last 20 years, total U.S. imports from all GSP-eligible developing countries has increased dramatically, from $123.2 billion in 1996 to a peak of $384 billion in 2008 (See **Figure 1**). Although this increase is significant, it is still a very small percentage of total U.S. imports. For example, in 2013, total imports from all GSP –eligible countries amounted to $277.0 billion, or about 12% of total U.S. imports of $2.2 trillion (imports for consumption, customs value). As

---

[78] Presidential Proclamation 8897 of June 27, 2013, 78 *Federal Register* 39949.

[79] See also "Outcomes of the 2012 GSP Annual Review" on the USTR website, http://www.ustr.gov/trade-topics/trade-development/preference-programs/generalized-system-preferences-gsp/current-review.

[80] 78 *Federal Register* 45596; 78 *Federal Register* 70091.

[81] P.L. 98-573, Section 501(b), 19 U.S.C. §2461 note. Additional factors are to allow for differences in developing countries; help developing countries generate foreign exchange reserves, further integrate developing countries into the international trading system; and encourage developing countries to eliminate trade barriers, guard intellectual property rights, provide worker rights; and address concerns of the United States with regard to adverse effects on U.S. producers and workers and compliance with GATT obligations.

Figure 1 illustrates, the percentage of imports entering the United States claiming the GSP preference in 2013 was even smaller, at about 1% of total U.S imports, and about 7% of total imports from GSP-eligible countries.[82]

The general growth trend in total imports from GSP countries over the time series could indicate, in very broad terms, that the GSP and other preferential programs may have helped create some export-driven growth in developing countries. In 2009, total imports from all GSP beneficiaries dropped to about $246 billion—most likely due to the global economic recession—but rebounded once again to $366 billion in 2011. Total imports entering duty-free under GSP also increased markedly from $17 billion in 1996 to a peak of $32 billion in 2008. In 2009, the value of goods entering under GSP fell to about $20 billion, and recovered slightly in 2010 to $23 billion. In 2011, the amount imported under GSP fell to $18.5 billion; increased slightly to $19.9 billion; and decreased again to $18.5 billion in 2013. The decrease in GSP imports since 2010 may be due to uncertainty based on GSP short-term program renewals, combined with GSP expiration between December 31, 2010, and November 2011 and from July 31, 2013, to the present. In addition, even if the GSP program is retroactively renewed (as generally is the case), additional paperwork is required in order to claim the preference, and if some importers decided not to submit the required documentation, a lower figure for GSP imports could result.

The percentage of goods entering the United States duty-free under the GSP program, relative to total U.S. imports from BDCs, ranged from 10% to12% from 2000 to 2007 (see **Figure 1**). Since 2008, the ratio of GSP imports to total BDC imports has decreased, from 8% in 2008 to a low of 5% in 2011. Factors that might contribute to keeping imports under the GSP program fairly low include CNLs, mandatory graduation, and uncertainty regarding program renewal. In addition, several consistent users of the preference have entered into FTAs with the United States, thus making them ineligible for GSP benefits.

---

[82] Tariffs on imports entering the United States are assessed retrospectively. Thus, despite the expiration of GSP on August 1, 2013, there is significant lag time in formal liquidation of imports claiming the GSP preference. Thus full-year GSP data for 2013 is available.

Figure 1. U.S. Imports from GSP Countries, 1996 - 2013

(billions of dollars)

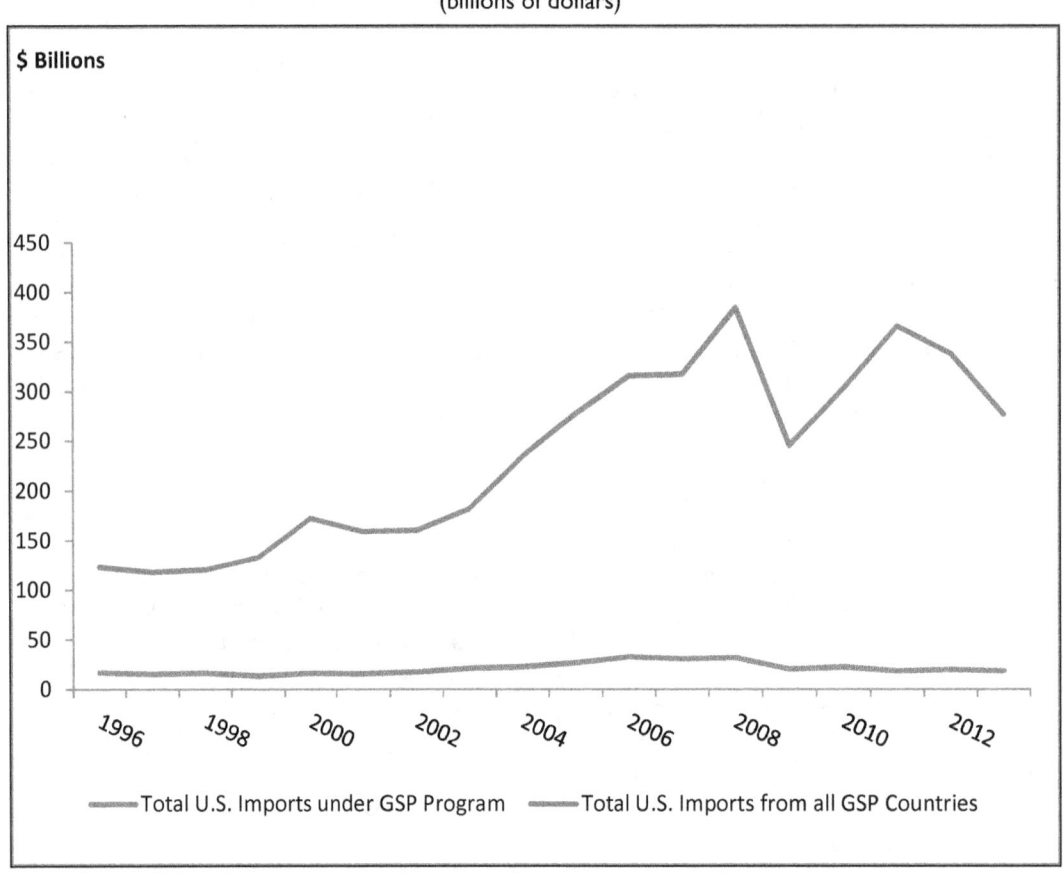

Source: USITC Trade Dataweb.

Another indicator of the GSP's impact on developing countries is the utilization rate of the preference. At first glance, it seems that only a few beneficiary developing countries use GSP to a great extent. However, as one study pointed out, the apparent lack of utilization masks the fact that many GSP-eligible goods may also be imported duty-free under other U.S. regional preference schemes, such as the African Growth and Opportunity Act (AGOA).[83] The study also illustrated that, for certain industries in BDCs, the positive impact of GSP is quite significant. For example, for all agricultural commodities eligible for GSP treatment, the GSP utilization rate was approximately 58%.[84]

Many developing countries with a natural competitive advantage in certain products use trade preferences such as the GSP to gain a foothold in the international market. For example, India and Thailand, two countries with well-established jewelry industries were able to expand their

---

[83] Organization for Economic Cooperation and Development (OECD). *Agriculture and Food.* Preferential Trading Arrangements in Agricultural and Food Markets The Case of the European Union and the United States: United States Preference Schemes. Volume 2005, No. 1, p. 81. See also U.S. Government Accountability Office. *U.S. Trade Preference Programs Provide Important Benefits, but a More Integrated Approach Would Better Ensure Programs Meet Shared Goals*, March 2008, p. 19.

[84] Ibid.

international reach through GSP programs and become competitive in the international market. However, some countries could also be encouraged by preferential programs to develop industry sectors in which they might not otherwise ever be able to compete, thus diverting resources from other industries that might actually become competitive over time (trade diversion).[85] Technically, one could argue that U.S. tariffs are trade barriers. GSP results in a removal of the trade barrier and allows GSP countries to grow industries where they have a comparative advantage.

Some economists assert that the lack of reciprocity in the GSP program could actually result in long-term costs for beneficiary countries. In multilateral trade negotiations, such as in the WTO Doha Development Round, countries may engage in reciprocal tariff reductions, meaning that all parties would agree to reduce their tariffs. By avoiding such reciprocal concessions, these economists say that developing countries are keeping in place protectionist trade policies that could actually impede their long-term growth. Moreover, these unilateral preferences could become an impediment to multilateral trade negotiations because developing country beneficiaries may prefer to seek ways of maintaining their unilateral preferences rather than exchanging them for reciprocal benefits.[86]

For this reason, some economists prefer multilateral, nondiscriminatory tariff cuts because preferential tariff programs, such as the GSP, can lead to inefficient production and trade patterns in developing countries.[87] When tariffs are reduced across-the-board, rather than in a preferential manner, countries tend to produce and export on the basis of their comparative advantage—thus exporting products that they produce relatively efficiently and importing products that others produce relatively efficiently. However, while some developing country producers (especially those whose products do not qualify under GSP) may benefit from multilateral tariff reductions, other industries may be hurt because their margin of preference under GSP is reduced.

Economic Effects on the U.S. Market

U.S. imports under the GSP program in 2013 were about $18.5 billion (see **Figure 1**) in comparison to total imports of about $2.2 trillion. This might indicate that the overall effects of GSP on the U.S. economy are quite small. In addition, most U.S. producers of import-competing products are largely protected from severe economic impact. First, certain products, such as most textile and apparel products, are designated "import sensitive" and therefore most are ineligible for duty-free treatment. Second, CNLs are triggered when imports of a product from a single country reach a specified threshold value, or when 50% of total U.S. imports of a product come from a single country.[88] Third, U.S. manufacturers or producers may petition the USTR to withdraw GSP benefits from a product if they are injured by the preference.[89]

---

[85] OECD, "Making Open Markets Work for Development," *Policy Brief*, October 2005, p. 2.

[86] Patrick Low, Roberta Piermartini, and Jurgen Richtering, *Multilateral Solutions to the Erosion of Non-Reciprocal Preferences in NAMA*, World Trade Organization, Economic Research and Statistics Division, Working Paper ERSD-2005-05, October 2005. R. E. Baldwin and T. Murray, "MFN Tariff Reductions and Developing Country Trade Benefits Under the GSP," *The Economic Journal*, vol. 87, no. 345 (March 1977), pp. 30-46.

[87] Bernard Herz and Marco Wagner, *The Dark Side of the Generalized System of Preferences*, German Council of Economic Experts, Working Paper 02/2010, February 2010, p. 27.

[88] 19 U.S.C. §2463(c).

[89] 15 C.F.R. 2007.0(b).

In federal budgetary terms, the Congressional Budget Office cost estimate for GSP based on H.R. 2832 (became P.L. 112-40, see **Table B-1**), the GSP program was projected to cost the United States $980 million in 2012 and $503 million in 2013 in foregone tariff revenues, which would be offset, in part, by an increase in import merchandise processing fees in 2017 to 2019.[90]

Some U.S. manufacturers and importers also benefit from the lower cost of consumer goods and raw materials imported under the GSP program. U.S. demand for certain individual products, such as jewelry, leather, and aluminum, is quite significant.[91] However, it is difficult to gauge, other than anecdotally, the overall impact of the GSP program on the U.S. market when compared to similar imports from other countries that do not receive the preference. It is possible that some merchandise entering under the GSP could be competitive even without the preference, but it is also possible that the duty-free status is the primary factor that has made imports from these countries, at least initially, more attractive.

Stakeholders' Concerns

Supporters of the GSP program include beneficiary developing country governments and exporters, U.S. importers, and some U.S. manufacturers who use inputs entering under GSP in downstream products. Some policymakers favor GSP renewal because they believe it is an important development and foreign policy tool. Those who oppose the program include some U.S. producers who manufacture competing products and some in Congress who favor more reciprocal approaches to trade policy. What follows is a thematic approach to the major topics of discussion in the GSP renewal debate.

"Special and Differential Treatment"

Developing countries have long maintained that "special and differential treatment," such as that provided by the GSP, is an important assurance of access to U.S. and other developed country markets in the midst of increasing globalization.[92] Many of these countries have built industries (or segments of industries) based on receiving certain tariff preferences.

Those who oppose automatic renewal of GSP have expressed the desire to see some "reciprocity" and "appreciation" on the part of BDCs—in the form of offers of improved market access—in return for renewal of the program.[93] Some of these policy makers reportedly favor continued progress in bilateral or multilateral negotiations in lieu of extending automatic, nonreciprocal benefits such as the GSP. Others have also charged that some of the more advanced BDCs have obstructed multilateral trade talks, especially in the WTO Doha Round.

---

[90] Congressional Budget Office, H.R. 2832, An Act to Extend the Generalized System of Preferences, and for Other Purposes, Cost Estimate, October 6, 2011, http://www.cbo.gov/sites/default/files/cbofiles/attachments/hr2832.pdf.

[91] In some product categories, imports under GSP account for 25% or more of total U.S. imports. For example, in 2013, 94% of copper stranded wire in HTS 7413.00.10; 76% of ferrochromium in HTS 7272.41.00; 72% of cocoa paste in HTS 1803.20.00; and 70% of plywood sheets of 6mm thick and under in HTS 4412.31.40 were imported under the GSP program.

[92] Women in International Trade (WIIT) event; "The Value of Attending a World Trade Organization Ministerial Conference," January 20, 2006.

[93] "Sen. Grassley Warns Brazil, India, on GSP; Stops Short of Predicting Graduation," *Inside U.S. Trade*, May 19, 2006.

Some Members have become more skeptical about the efficacy of any further trade concessions as they hear from constituents about lost jobs and other domestic hardships attributed to various factors, including the recent economic downturn in the U.S. economy.[94] Other Members assert that extension and expansion of these programs "will send a signal to developing countries that we will stand with them as they grow."[95]

Erosion of Preferential Margins

Developing countries have expressed concern about the overall progressive erosion[96] of preferential margins as a result of across-the-board tariff negotiations within the context of multilateral trade negotiations such as the Doha Round. In 1997, a study prepared by the Organization for Economic Cooperation and Development (OECD) found that the degree of erosion of preferences resulting from Uruguay Round (1986-1994) tariff concessions by the Quad countries (Canada, European Union, Japan, United States) was indeed significant.[97] Some economists point out that if multilateral rounds of tariff reductions, combined with the proliferation of bilateral and regional trade agreements continue, the preference may disappear completely unless GSP tariff headings are expanded to include more "import-sensitive" products.[98]

One example of present concern of preference erosion is the aforementioned group of business and NGO groups that have proposed providing duty-free, quota-free (DFQF) U.S. market access to all least-developed countries. However, many sub-Saharan African countries have expressed concern that an approach like this could place them in direct competition for U.S. market share with other developing countries, thus diluting the value of the preferential treatment that they receive through the African Growth and Opportunity Act (AGOA).[99]

Other economists say that preference erosion could be more than outweighed by the benefits of increased market access, even for developing countries, brought about by multilateral trade liberalization.[100] These economists say that, rather than continuing GSP and other preferential programs (either through inertia or concern that removing them would be seen as "acting against"

---

[94] Washington International Trade Association (WITA) event; "The 2006 Congressional Trade Agenda," February 15, 2006.

[95] "Rangel Bill Would Extend Trade Benefits for Developing Countries," Press Release, March 30, 2006.

[96] While overall multilateral preferences may be eroding, the tariff benefits for individual items is still quite significant. For example, the U.S. tariff on flashlights (eligible for duty-free access for all BDCs) is 12.5% *ad valorem*. Some GSP-eligible jewelry items have tariffs as high as 13.5%.

[97] Organization for International Cooperation and Development, *Market Access for the Least-Developed Countries: Where are the Obstacles?* Published by World Trade Organization, WT/LDC/HL/19, October 21, 1997, Table 12, p. 47. The study estimated that in 1997, the loss in the Canadian market was approximately 71%, in the EU 26%, in Japan 34%, and in the United States, 50% (hereinafter OECD study).

[98] Sanchez Arnau, Juan C. *The Generalized System of Preferences and the World Trade Organization*, London: Cameron May, Ltd., 2002, p. 282.

[99] Alliance to End Hunger, et al. Letter to House Ways and Means and Senate Finance Chairs and Ranking Members, April 22, 2009. African Ambassador's Group Statement, May 13, 2013.

[100] Baldwin, R.E. and Murray, T. "MFN Tariff Reductions and Developing Country Trade Benefits Under the GSP," *Economic Journal* 87:345, March 1977, p. 46.

the world's poorest populations), a better approach might be to "assist them in addressing the constraints that really underlie their sluggish trade and growth performance."[101]

Under-Utilization of GSP

Some who oppose the GSP program say that the proportionately small amount of trade entering under GSP means that the program is underused, and therefore easily eliminated. Some supporters agree that this is especially true for many least-developed country beneficiaries, who historically are not large users of the preference.

Others have suggested that the GSP may not be used by some countries because they are unfamiliar with the program, because some BDC governments do a poor job of promoting the existence of available opportunities under the preference, because of the lack of available infrastructure (for example, undeveloped or damaged roads and ports that impede the efforts to get goods into the international market), because many products developing countries are able to produce are deemed "import sensitive," or a combination of all of these factors.[102] One option for addressing these factors could be assistance through U.S. trade capacity building efforts.

Trade as Foreign Assistance

No other U.S. preference program is more broadly based or encompasses as many countries as GSP. As a result, the program is supported by many observers who believe that it is an effective, low-cost means of providing economic assistance to developing countries. They maintain that encouraging trade by private companies through the GSP stimulates economic development much more effectively than intergovernmental aid and other means of assistance.[103] Economic development assistance through trade is a long-standing element of U.S. policy, and other trade promotion programs such as the AGOA and the Caribbean Basin Trade Partnership Act (CBTPA) are also based on this premise.

Conditionality of Preferences

Some supporters of GSP and other non-reciprocal programs assert that the conditions required (such as worker rights and IPR requirements) for GSP qualification provide the United States with international political leverage that can be used to preserve U.S. foreign and commercial interests.[104] However, some beneficiary countries actively object to these "country practice" provisions and regard them as penalties. Some countries (such as Brazil and India) that have been targeted for GSP eligibility review in the past perceive that such action indicates that they are being penalized for advocating for their own national development goals in multilateral talks.[105]

---

[101] OECD study, p. 27.

[102] U.S. General Accountability Office. *International Trade: U.S. Trade Preference Programs Provide Important Benefits, But a More Integrated Approach Would Better Ensure that Programs Meet Shared Goals.* GAO 08-443, March 2008., pp.33-35 (hereinafter 2008 GAO Report).

[103] September 21, 2006 DC Bar meeting.

[104] The Coalition for GSP. *The U.S. Generalized System of Preferences Program: An Integral Part of the U.S. Economy*, January 1997, p. 3.

[105] September 6, 2006 public comment letter to USTR from ActionAid International USA.

Some U.S. intellectual property industry representatives, labor groups, and other constituencies oppose what they perceive to be the U.S. Administration's inconsistent enforcement of these provisions. For example, one group expressed that they were "shocked and dumbfounded" that GSP eligibility is being renewed annually for such countries as Brazil, Russia, and Venezuela in spite of IPR violations.[106] This domestic opposition may indicate that, at times, that GSP as a tool is of limited usefulness. According to the USTR, however, U.S. officials favor working with beneficiary countries during country practice reviews to actively address compliance issues before removing a country from eligibility. Between 2001 and 2006, one country, Ukraine, was removed from eligibility for GSP because of IPR concerns, but was reinstated a few years later after taking steps to resolve the problem.[107]

Lower Costs of Imports

U.S. importers of goods who import components, parts, or materials duty-free under the GSP maintain that the preference results in lower costs for these intermediate goods which, in turn, can make U.S. firms more competitive and be passed on to consumers. For example, the Coalition for GSP, a group of U.S. companies and associations in support of GSP, asserted that the program saved American companies $749 million on $19.9 billion in imports in 2012.[108] The same group claims that the expiration of GSP has cost American companies "nearly $2 million per day in higher taxes while waiting for Congress to renew the program."[109]

Even though most U.S. producers are shielded by the automatic CNL "safeguards" triggered by increased imports under the GSP, U.S. manufacturers and workers are sometimes adversely affected by the program due to CNL waivers.[110] For example, in 2010, Exxel Outdoors, a U.S. company that manufactures certain non-down sleeping bags, petitioned for their removal from GSP eligibility, claiming that their business operations were being harmed by imports of duty-free sleeping bags from Bangladesh under the GSP program.[111] These sleeping bag categories were ultimately removed from GSP duty-free treatment in January 2012.[112] However, results of U.S. manufacturers have not always been successful. For example, in 2004, three U.S. producers of titanium complained that the then-Bush Administration refused to terminate duty-free market access for wrought titanium (ordinarily subject to a 15% duty assessment), despite a petition asking the government not to waive the import limits. Imports of Russian titanium were allowed to continue to enter the United States duty-free under the presidential waiver even though its sales made up more than 60% of U.S. imports of that product.[113]

---

[106] "Grassley Throws Up Obstacle to Trade-Preference Renewal," *Congress Daily*, September 18, 2006.

[107] United States Government Accountability Office, *U.S. Trade Preference Programs: An Overview of Use by Beneficiaries and U.S. Administrative Reviews*, GAO-07-1209, September 2007, p. 4.

[108] Coalition for GSP website, http://www.tradepartnership.com/site/gsp.html.

[109] Letter from Coalition for GSP to Members of House and Senate, January 28, 2014, http://renewgsptoday.com.

[110] 19 U.S.C. §2463(c).

[111] "Sleeping Bags Removed from GSP after USTR Administrative Review," *Inside U.S. Trade*, January 5, 2012.

[112] 77 *Federal Register* 1549, January 10, 2012.

[113] "Administration Decides to Keep Russian GSP Benefits for Titanium," *Inside U.S. Trade,* July 9, 2004.

Conclusion and Options for Congress

The U.S. GSP program, as established by Title V of the Trade Act of 1974 was last extended through July 31, 2013, in P.L. 112-40, for all GSP beneficiary countries not covered by the African Growth and Opportunity Act (AGOA).[114] The African Growth and Opportunity Acceleration Act of 2004 (P.L. 108-274) had previously authorized an extension of GSP preferences for all beneficiary developing sub-Saharan African countries under AGOA through September 30, 2015. Therefore, whether or not the GSP program is renewed with respect to other countries, GSP benefits will continue to be extended to all AGOA countries until that date.[115]

Several options are available to Congress with respect to the treatment of the GSP program. As explained more fully below, Congress could allow the GSP program to expire, support reciprocal tariff and market access benefits through FTAs, renew the GSP for least-developed beneficiaries only, renew the existing program for all beneficiaries without major amendments, or extend the program in a modified form. Although the GSP is a unilateral and non-reciprocal tariff preference, any changes to the program would need to be considered in light of the requirements of the WTO Enabling Clause, as it has been interpreted by the WTO Appellate Body. At a minimum, the United States would need to notify—and possibly consult with—other WTO members regarding any withdrawal or modification of GSP benefits, as required by paragraph 4 of the Enabling Clause.[116] The United States could also pursue a WTO waiver were any modifications of the GSP program considered not to comport fully with U.S. WTO obligations.

Suspend GSP

The GSP statute automatically expired for all beneficiary developing countries (except for AGOA-eligible countries) on July 31, 2013.[117] No legislative action would be required if Congress desired to permanently suspend the program.

At the same time, supporters of the GSP program assert that it is as important for many domestic manufacturers and importers as for the countries that receive the preferential access for their products. Some U.S. industry sectors, such as the automobile industry, could be adversely impacted by suspension of GSP, due to the dependence on duty-free (thus lower-cost) manufacturing inputs imported under the preference, such as brake parts, vehicle transmissions, and tires. In addition, they say that small and medium businesses are disproportionately affected because they are less able to adjust to increased costs of factors of production due to GSP.[118] On the other hand, some U.S. manufacturers of import-competing products might, at least marginally, benefit.

---

[114] As of January 1, 2012, there are 38 AGOA beneficiaries.

[115] 19 U.S.C. §2466b, as amended by Section 7 of the AGOA Acceleration Act of 2004 (P.L. 108-274).

[116] Paragraph 4 states that any contracting party that grants a preferential program and seeks to modify or withdraw it must notify the other contracting parties, give them adequate time and opportunity to discuss any difficulties, and help them to reach satisfactory solutions. See http://www.wto.org/english/docs_e/legal_e/enabling1979_e.htm.

[117] 19 U.S.C. §2465.

[118] Coalition for GSP, "American Companies Frustrated by Congress' Inability to Renew Generalized System of Preferences Program," press release, August 1, 2013, http://renewgsptoday.com/.

Other observers indicate that if GSP were allowed to expire, or be otherwise modified through country graduation or limitations on CNL or other waivers, these actions might also weaken the hand of U.S. negotiators because GSP could no longer be used as an incentive for participation in negotiations. Many developing nations already perceive the United States as generally unwilling to accept multilateral efforts to grant additional "special and differential treatment" for developing country WTO members unless reciprocal concessions for improved market access are made for U.S. products.[119] They say that GSP expiration could cause the negotiating positions of developing countries to harden, rather than soften, as they seek to make up for these lost benefits through the negotiations.[120]

The United States could also lose leverage in addressing certain trade-related foreign policy and development requirements enacted in the GSP law that beneficiary nations must be willing to accept in order to retain GSP eligibility. If the GSP program was not reauthorized, the ability to encourage these practices through the GSP review process, and other means afforded by GSP eligibility, would no longer be available.[121]

Negotiate Free-Trade Agreements with GSP Countries

Some observers have suggested that the GSP should be abandoned in favor of FTAs or regional trading arrangements (RTAs) that would provide reciprocal trade benefits for the United States. Such arrangements could provide additional markets for U.S. exports, as well as stimulate the growth of industries in developing-country trading partners. Since these tariff concessions under these agreements would apply to more sectors of the economy than GSP, FTAs might increase the likelihood of across-the-board economic stimulation. In fact, each one of the United States' current FTA partners, with the exception of Canada, was at one time a beneficiary of the GSP program.[122] Arguably, these FTA partners have benefited more from the FTA than they did from GSP.

Authorize GSP Only for Least-Developed Countries

Some in Congress favor modifying the GSP so that the benefits apply only to least-developed beneficiaries. This option seems to be in line with the changes that the EU and Canada have made to their GSP programs. Since many African least-developed beneficiaries[123] will continue to receive the GSP preference until mid-2015 under AGOA, an LDC-only GSP extension, at least in the short term, would benefit the following LDCs: Afghanistan, Bhutan, Cambodia, Central

---

[119] OECD GSP Review, p. 11.

[120] Ibid.

[121] For more information on the GSP review process, see 15 C.F.R. §2007.0.

[122] Some U.S. FTA partners were GSP beneficiaries at the time FTA implementing legislation was enacted. Singapore and South Korea were graduated from GSP in 1989, and thus were not GSP beneficiaries at the time the United States implemented their respective FTAs. Israel retained GSP status until 1995, and Jordan still enjoys GSP status. Implementing language for all other FTAs stated that "the President shall terminate the designation of ... as a beneficiary developing country for the purposes of title V of the Trade Act of 1974 on the date of entry into force of the Agreement."

[123] These least-developed AGOA countries are: Angola, Benin, Burkina Faso, Burundi, Chad, Comoros, Djibouti, Ethiopia, The Gambia, Guinea, Lesotho, Liberia, Malawi, Mali, Mauritania, Mozambique, Niger, Rwanda, Sao Tome and Principe, Senegal, Sierra Leone, South Sudan, Tanzania, Togo, Uganda, and Zambia.

African Republic, Congo (Kinshasa), Haiti,[124] Kiribati, Madagascar, Nepal, Samoa, the Solomon Islands, Somalia, Timor-Leste, Tuvalu, Vanuatu, and Yemen.[125] Of these countries, three—Angola, Cambodia, and the Solomon Islands—were the LDCs that made the most use of the GSP (by value) in 2013. Arguably, U.S. efforts through trade capacity building could help other LDCs take greater advantage of the preference.

Modify GSP

Another possible approach for Congress would be to modify the Generalized System of Preferences scheme as it applies to all beneficiary developing countries, including least-developed countries. Some of these options could have the effect of expanding the GSP program, while others could serve to restrict its application.

Expand Application of GSP

Were Congress to expand or enhance application of the GSP, the following options could be considered:

- Expand the list of tariff lines permitted duty-free access. Allow some "import sensitive" products (in which developing countries often have a competitive advantage) to receive preferential access.

- Improve rule of origin requirements to provide more predictability. Current rules provide no measurable definition of "substantial transformation." Thus, U.S. officials often make eligibility decisions on a case-by-case basis. Thus, BDCs sometimes have no predictable way of knowing before shipment whether certain foreign components are eligible for GSP treatment under the 35% domestic content requirement.[126]

- Eliminate competitive need limitations for BDCs, or raise the thresholds that trigger them.

- Revise and expand eligibility requirements.

Restrict Application of Preferences

The following is a list of possible approaches if Congress desired to extend, but further restrict, imports under the GSP:

- Reconsider criteria for graduation of countries from GSP, or strengthen the provision that allows graduation of individual industry sectors within beneficiary countries. For example, the President could be required to grant BDC status only if a country (1) complies with all mandatory requirements and (2) has a per-capita income below a certain level.

---

[124] Haiti was provided additional unilateral preferences through the Haiti Economic Lift Act of 2010 (P.L. 111-171). CRS Report RL34687, *The Haitian Economy and the HOPE Act*, by J. F. Hornbeck.

[125] The Central African Republic, Congo (Kinshasa), Guinea-Bissau, Madagascar, and Somalia, are not designated as beneficiary AGOA countries in 2014, but retain their GSP eligibility.

[126] 2008 GAO Report, p. 55.

- Modify the rules of origin requirement for qualifying products to require that a greater percentage of the direct costs of processing operations (currently 35%)[127] originate in beneficiary developing countries.

- Lower the threshold at which the President may (or must) withdraw, suspend, or limit the application of duty-free treatment of certain products (CNLs).[128]

- Require the President to more frequently and actively monitor (currently an annual process) the economic progress of beneficiary countries, as well as compliance with GSP criteria.

- Add additional eligibility criteria; for example, to include movement toward sustainable development or environmental preservation.

---

[127] 19 U.S.C. §2463(a)(2)(A)(ii)(II). The statute further specifies that a product may be made in one BDC or any two or more such countries that are members of the same designated association of countries. For beneficiary countries under AGOA, this percentage may also include up to 15% (as to value) of U.S. origin (19 U.S.C. §2466a(b)(2)).

[128] 19 U.S.C. §2463(c).

Appendix A. Leading U.S. GSP Product Imports

Table A-1. Leading U.S. GSP Product Imports, 2013

Harmonized Tariff Schedule Subheading	General NTR Tariff Rate	Description	Value of Imports Under GSP ($ millions)
27090020	10.5 cents per barrel	Petroleum oils and oils from bituminous minerals, crude, testing 25 degrees A.P.I. or more	$623
40111010	4%	New pneumatic radial tires, of rubber, of a kind used on motor cars (including station wagons and racing cars)	$341
72024100	1.9%	Ferrochromium containing by weight more than 4% of carbon	$319
76061230	3%	Aluminum alloy, plates/sheets/strip, with thickness over 0.2mm, rectangular (incl. square), not clad	$266
84159080	1.4%	Parts for air conditioning machines, not otherwise specified or indicated	$262
40151910	3%	Seamless gloves of vulcanized rubber other than hard rubber, other than surgical or medical gloves	$229
10059040	0.25 cents per kilogram	Corn (maize), other than seed and yellow dent corn	$212
21069099	6.4%	Food preparations not elsewhere specified or included, not canned or frozen	$209
68029900	6.5%	Monumental or building stone and articles thereof, not otherwise specified or indicated, further worked than simply cut/sawn	$196
22029090	0.2 cents per liter	Nonalcoholic beverages, not otherwise specified or indicated, not including fruit or vegetable juices of heading 2009	$185
71131929	5.5%	Gold necklaces and neck chains (o/than of rope or mixed links)	$180
72023000	3.9%	Ferrosilicon manganese	$172
72022150	1.5%	Ferrosilicon containing by weight more than 55% but not more than 80% of silicon, not otherwise specified or indicated	$164
44123140	8%	Plywood sheets not over 6mm thick, with specified tropical wood outer ply, not surface-covered	$142

Harmonized Tariff Schedule Subheading	General NTR Tariff Rate	Description	Value of Imports Under GSP ($ millions)
17049035	5.6%	Sugar confections or sweetmeats ready for consumption, not containing cocoa, other than candied nuts or cough drops	$138
		Subtotal Above:	$3,648
		All Other:	$14,868
		Total:	$18,516

Source: USITC Trade Dataweb, http://dataweb.usitc.gov, and Harmonized Tariff Schedule, 2009.

Notes: Imports for consumption, actual U.S. dollars. Tariff rates are *ad valorem* unless otherwise specified. NTR stands for "normal trade relations," which in U.S. law replaces the term "most-favored-nation."

Table A-2. Leading GSP Beneficiaries and Total, 2013

Rank	Beneficiary Developing Country	GSP Duty-Free Imports ($ millions)	Total Imports ($ millions)
1	India	4,223	41,459
2	Thailand	3,341	26,089
3	Brazil	2,307	26,861
4	Indonesia	1,834	18,776
5	Philippines	1,268	9,239
6	Turkey	1,213	6,557
7	South Africa	1,090	8,395
8	Angola	710	8,902
9	Russia[a]	466	25,931
10	Pakistan	225	3,666
11	Ecuador	183	11,454
12	Sri Lanka	158	2,382
13	Bolivia	158	1,288
14	Tunisia	146	736
15	Venezuela	110	27,036
Imports from Top 15 Beneficiaries		17,433	218,770
All Other Beneficiaries		1,083	58,180
Total Imports from all Beneficiaries		18,516	276,950

Source: USITC Trade Dataweb, http://dataweb.usitc.gov.

a. On May 7, 2014, President Obama notified Congress that he intended to remove Russia from the GSP program.

Appendix B. GSP Implementation and Renewal

Table B-1. GSP Implementation and Renewal, 1974-2013

Public Law	Effective Date	Date Expired	Notes
P.L. 93-618, Title V, Trade Act of 1974	January 2, 1975	January 2, 1985	Statute originally enacted.
P.L. 98-573, Title V, Trade and Tariff Act of 1984	October 30, 1984	July 4, 1993	Substantially amended and restated.
P.L. 103-66, Section 13802 (in Omnibus Budget Reconciliation Act, 1993)	August 10, 1993	September 30, 1994	Extended retroactively from July 5, 1993 to August 10, 1993. Also struck out reference to "Union of Soviet Socialist Republics"
P.L. 103-465, Section 601 Uruguay Round Agreements Act	December 8, 1994	July 31, 1995	Extended retroactively from September 30, 1994 to December 8, 1994. No other amendments to provision.
P.L. 104-188, Subtitle J, Section 1952 GSP Renewal Act of 1996 (in Small Business Job Protection Act of 1996)	October 1, 1996 (for GSP renewal only)	May 31, 1997	Substantially amended and restated. Extended retroactively from August 1, 1995 to October 1, 1996.
P.L. 105-34, Subtitle H, Section 981 (in Taxpayer Relief Act of 1997)	August 5, 1997	June 30, 1998	Extended retroactively from May 31, 1997 to August 5, 1997. No other amendments to provision.
P.L. 105-277, Subtitle B, Section 101 (in Omnibus Consolidated and Emergency Supplemental Appropriations, 1999)	October 21, 1998	June 30, 1999	Extended retroactively from July 1, 1998 to October 21, 1998. No other amendments to provision.
P.L. 106-170, Section 508, (in Ticket to Work and Work Incentives Act of 1999)	December 17, 1999	September 30, 2001	Extended retroactively from July 1, 1999 to December 17, 1999. No other amendments to provision.
P.L. 107-210, Division D, Title XLI Trade Act of 2002	August 6, 2002	December 31, 2006	Extended retroactively from September 30, 2001, to August 6, 2002. Amended to (1) include requirement that BDCs take steps to support efforts of United States to combat terrorism and (2) further define the term "internationally recognized worker rights."
P.L. 109-432, Title VIII	December 31, 2006	December 31, 2008	Extended before program lapse.
P.L. 110-436, Section 4	October 16, 2008	December 31, 2009	Extended before program lapse.

Public Law	Effective Date	Date Expired	Notes
P.L. 111-124	December 28, 2009	December 31, 2010	Extended before program lapse.
P.L. 112-40	November 5, 2011	July 31, 2013	Extended retroactively from December 31, 2010 to November 5, 2011.

Source: CRS analysis using the Legislative Information System (LIS).

Appendix C. GSP Beneficiary Countries

Table C-1.Beneficiary Developing Countries and Regions for Purposes of the Generalizes System of Preferences

(as of January 2014)

Independent Countries

Afghanistan[A+]	Egypt	Madagascar[A+]	Seychelles
A bania	Eritrea	Malawi[A+]	Sierra Leone[A+]
Algeria	Ethiopia [A+]	Maldives	Solomon Islands [A+]
Angola[A+]	Fiji	Mali[A+]	Somalia[A+]
Armenia	Gabon	Mauritania[A+]	South Africa
Azerbaijan	Gambia, The[A+]	Mauritius	South Sudan [A+]
Belize	Georgia	Moldova	Sri Lanka
Benin[A+]	Ghana	Mongolia	Suriname
Bhutan[A+]	Grenada	Montenegro	Swaziland
Bolivia	Guinea[A+]	Mozambique[A+]	Tanzania[A+]
Bosnia and Hercegovina	Guinea-Bissau[A+]	Namibia	Thailand
Botswana	Guyana	Nepal[A+]	Timor-Leste [A+]
Brazil	Haiti[A+]	Niger[A+]	Togo[A+]
Burkina Faso[A+]	India	Nigeria	Tonga
Burundi[A+]	Indonesia	Pakistan	Tunisia
Cambodia[A+]	Iraq	Papua New Guinea	Turkey
Cameroon	Jamaica	Paraguay	Tuvalu[A+]
Cape Verde	Jordan	Philippines	Uganda[A+]
Central African Republic[A+]	Kazakhstan	Russia	Ukraine
Chad[A+]	Kenya	Rwanda[A+]	Uruguay
Comoros[A+]	Kiribati[A+]	St. Kitts and Nevis	Uzbekistan
Congo (Brazzaville)	Kosovo	Saint Lucia	Vanuatu[A+]
Congo (Kinshasa) [A+]	Kyrgyzstan	Saint Vincent and the Grenadines	Venezuela
Cote d'Ivoire	Lebanon	Samoa[A+]	Republic of Yemen[A+]
Djibouti[A+]	Lesotho[A+]	Sao Tome and Principe[A+]	Zambia[A+]
Dominica	Liberia[A+]	Senegal	Zimbabwe
Ecuador	Macedonia, Former Yugoslav Republic of	Serbia	

Non-Independent Countries and Territories Eligible for GSP Benefits

Anguilla	Heard Island and McDonald Islands	Tokelau
British Indian Ocean Territory	Montserrat	Virgin Islands, British
Christmas Island (Australia)	Niue	Wallis and Fortuna
Cocos (Keeling) Islands	Norfolk Island	West Bank and Gaza Strip
Cook Islands	Pitcairn Islands	Western Sahara
Falkland Islands (Islas Malvinas)	Saint Helena	

Associations of Countries (treated as one country) Eligible for GSP Benefits

Member Countries of the Cartagena Agreement (Andean Group)	Qualifying Member Countries of the Association of South East Asian Nations (ASEAN)	Qualifying Member Countries of the Caribbean Common Market (CARICOM)
Bolivia	Cambodia	Belize
Ecuador	Indonesia	Dominica
Venezuela	Philippines	Grenada
	Thailand	Guyana
		Jamaica
		Montserrat
		St. Kitts and Nevis
		Saint Lucia
		Saint Vincent and the Grenadines

Member Countries of the West African Economic and Monetary Union (WAEMU)	Qualifying Member Countries of the Southern Africa Development Community (SADC)
Benin	Botswana
Burkina Faso	Mauritius
Cote d'Ivoire	Tanzania
Guinea-Bissau	
Mali	
Niger	
Senegal	
Togo	

Qualifying Member Countries of the South Asian Association for Regional Cooperation (SAARC)
Afghanistan
Bangladesh
Bhutan
India
Nepal
Pakistan
Sri Lanka

Source: Harmonized Tariff Schedule, January 2013.

Note: A+ indicates Least-Developed Countries.

Author Contact Information

Vivian C. Jones
Specialist in International Trade and Finance
vcjones@crs.loc.gov, 7-7823